Leave a Light On
Prayers for a Prodigal

RAE ANN HOUSTON

Jackson Creek Media Group, Inc.

Leave a Light On
Prayers for a Prodigal

Copyright 2017
By Rae Ann Houston / Author

All rights reserved. No part of this publication may be reproduced, stored in a retrieval system, or transmitted in any form or by any means—electronic, mechanical, digital, photocopy, recording, or any other—except for brief quotations in printed reviews, without the prior written permission of the author and publisher.
Printed in the United States of America

ISBN: 978-0-9759319-6-7 (13 digit)
      0-9759319-6-2 (9 digit)

Jackson Creek Media Group, Inc.

Dedication

I dedicate this book to the Triune God:
1) The Most High God, Yahweh. The God who sees and who is the Alpha and the Omega. He is in control of all time and space and doesn't ever miss a thing;
2) The Son of God, Jesus Christ who is our Messiah and Redeemer and who is ever interceding on our behalf;
3) The Holy Spirit who indwells us continually guiding us as we seek to shine God's light in our dark world.

Acknowledgement

I want to thank my daughter, Ashley Tilford, who encouraged me continually on this project and diligently critiqued it. I owe a debt of appreciation to my loving husband, Jay Houston, who made all of the editorial changes possible. Also I want to thank my dear friends Brenda Richards and Sherry LeMaster who kept cheering me on to complete this endeavor for God's glory.

Introduction

The day is beautiful: clear skies with a light breeze. The porch light is on so someone coming to your home will know which place is yours. Then all of a sudden, the skies grow dark and the wind picks up. Dark clouds are rolling in and you hear thunder in the distance. The porch light continues to shine even as the rain starts pouring in sheets and the winds begin to rage. What brought on this horrible storm? There didn't seem to be any warning or expectation. But still that light on the porch provides a beacon of hope to anyone stuck out in the messy weather.

That same scenario can play out in life. You dedicated your child to the Lord, taught him/her how to fear God and respect people...all those things that are right in the sight of God. You were shining in their life like a beacon of light and hope in the dark world you were protecting them from. Your little one grew and developed as a 'normal' kid and then into adulthood. All of a sudden, when you least expected it, they rebelled. They were no longer interested in things they were taught. They wanted to find their 'own path'. They were trying to find their way without the Lord's guidance.

Perhaps you have a spouse, dear friend, neighbor, sibling, or parent; someone you trusted completely – confided in, someone you grew up with in the same home, with the same parents but something has happened. They have changed. They are not living a lifestyle that is pleasing to God anymore. You thought your relationship was built on solid Biblical principles, but now they have turned away, don't want to hear and don't talk about their faith anymore. They have left their faith behind. How can you help them?? What do you do next??

God's word to you today,
right now...
in this moment...is this:
Don't give up on them.
Don't turn the light out and walk away.
Wait for His timing in their lives and in yours.
Leave a light on throughout your life constantly.

This daily devotional is designed to assist you in focusing on how to be a light in the darkness. The Apostle Luke challenges us in Luke 11:33: "No one lights a lamp and puts it on a place where it will be hidden or under a bowl. **Instead he puts it on the stand so that those who come in may see the light."**

Just as the father of the prodigal son from Luke 15 waited and watched eagerly for the prodigal to return...so must we always remain hopeful and ever vigilant for opportunities to show love to our prodigal. Personally, my own two children seriously questioned their faith and God's plan for their lives in their young adulthood. Thankfully, through God's grace and many fervent prayers they are now both actively following hard after God and His plan for each of their lives.

It is my prayer that this devotional will give you refreshing examples of how to pray for and act toward your prodigal. Each day begins with a personal time of prayer and meditation. This is a time to focus your thoughts on a specific topic, followed by scripture and words of encouragement. At the end of each day's devotion is a prayer for your prodigal and a life verse you can memorize specific to the topic of the day. Throughout this devotional this blank (___) is added so you can insert your prodigal's name into the prayers to make them more personal.

Throughout the book are pages entitled *"Personal Prayers and Thoughts."* These are set aside for you to record your thoughts and conversations with God. Be sure to record the date of those prayers and leave room for answered prayers, either answered with a yes/positive answer or a no/not now answer. For more information on practical prayer journaling tips, please see www.beaconofhopedevotion.com.

It is important to note that as you pray through this devotional, you may not see or notice any immediate changes in your prodigal. But through consistent prayer, persistent love and constant trust in God, you can continue to let His light shine through you brightly. It might take months or years to see any difference but God will use you to shine His light into their lives.

"And this is my prayer: that your love may abound more and more in knowledge and depth of insight, so that you may be able to discern what is best and may be pure and blameless until the day of Christ, filled with the fruit of righteousness that comes through Jesus Christ – to the glory and praise of God." Philippians 1:9-11

Let your light shine…

Day 1
Leave a Light On

Meditation Moment and Prayer:
Lord I acknowledge my need to be a light, but it's so hard. I am so discouraged and worried. Please use this book and specifically this day to give me hope and a new motivation to leave a light on through my life for (___).

Remember this:
Do not give up on them.
Leave a light on throughout your life constantly.

Luke 15:11-32 gives us an excellent example of a heartbroken parent waiting and watching for his prodigal son. "Jesus continued: "There was a man who had two sons. The younger one said to his father, "Father, give me my share of the estate." So he divided his property between them.
"Not long after that, the younger son got together all he had, set off for a distant country and there squandered his wealth in wild living. After he had spent everything, there was a severe famine in that whole country, and he began to be in need. So he went and hired himself out to a citizen of that country, who sent him to his fields to feed pigs. He longed to fill his stomach with the pods that the pigs were eating but no one gave him anything.
"When he came to his senses, he said, 'How many of my father's hired men have food to spare, and here I am starving to death! I will set out and go back to my father and say to him: Father, I have sinned against heaven and against you. I am no longer worthy to be called your son; make me like one of your hired men. So he got up and

went to his father.

"But while he was still a long way off, his father saw him and was filled with compassion for him; he ran to his son, threw his arms around him and kissed him.

"The son said to him, 'Father, I have sinned against heaven and against you. I am no longer worthy to be called your son.'

"But the father said to his servants, 'Quick! Bring the best robe and put it on him. Put a ring on his finger and sandals on his feet. Bring the fattened calf and kill it. Let's have a feast and celebrate. For this son of mine was dead and is alive again; he was lost and is found.' (Luke 15:11-24)

The prodigal story states "while he was still a long way off, his father saw him and was filled with compassion for him...." The father was ever vigilant, always looking, hoping and praying his son would return home safely. The father was on the lookout for him even though there had probably been no 'word' from him in a long time. They didn't have cell phones, Facebook or social media back in those days to 'keep tabs' on their loved ones.

Just imagine being in that father's shoes. I'm sure he watched daily, scanning the horizon in all directions but especially the direction the son had left in. He was just waiting for another glimpse of his young son. I am sure you can understand how he must have felt. These are some of the thoughts and feelings you may have experienced many times as well:

1. Disbelief – can this truly be happening?
2. Anger - how dare he/she behave like this?
3. Gut wrenching worry – what could they be doing now? Are they safe?
4. Never ending hope for their safe return – will they come home tonight?

Perhaps the Father asked about the son every time he went into town or had a villager pass his way:
"Have you seen my son?"
"Have you heard how he's doing, who he's working for?"
He might ask the shopkeepers, the local farmers, the rabbi and holy men of the community…"What news have you heard about my child?"

You know the drill!! You are constantly on the lookout. You are constantly wondering and praying all is ok and that the heart of **your** prodigal would turn back toward God.

The choices your prodigal makes are <u>**their**</u> responsibility. But your response to the prodigal in their choices is <u>**your**</u> responsibility. Are you tempted to give up hoping and watching? Or are you willing to be like the father, willing to accept them back with open arms?

        Let this be an encouragement to you.
Don't give up on them.
Leave a light on continuously through your life.

Praying for the prodigal:
Lord, in this moment of worry and fear, I choose to praise you for (___). He/she is fearfully and wonderfully made in your image. I praise you for (___) (List three positive attributes of _____.) Help me focus on these positive things throughout today as they come to my mind. In this way, may I be Your light in their darkness. Help me choose to respond to (___) in love. I want to be willing to accept them back with open arms.

Life verse:
"Devote yourselves to prayer, being watchful and thankful…" Colossians 4:2

Day 2
How to Become a Brighter Light

Meditation Moment and Prayer:
Lord, I understand that as believers we are to be a light in this dark world but I don't even know where to begin. I am looking for guidance and direction as I try to muddle through this unbelievable nightmare. Please show me ways through this time on how I can learn to trust You and look to You for guidance. Help me be a brighter light even when the storms seem to be relentless.

Here is something to help you remember how to become a brighter light for Christ in our dark world:
L-Lift Prayers Continually
I-Illuminate the darkness with God's Word
G-Generously give unconditional love
H-Have an expectant heart
T-Trust God to accomplish HIS work in HIS timing

This is where you start the quest of becoming more like Jesus to your prodigal. You must first make the conscious decision that your prodigal is in God's hands. He/she is not in their situation by mistake or accident. God is using everything that touches them for His purpose, their growth and His glory. This is where you begin. You must be willing to trust in that fact…God has this. And …it's going to be okay.

Often we get stuck remembering the past hurts and mistakes. We get stuck in a rut thinking that nothing will ever mend all of this mess. Start now believing in change.

Prayer for the prodigal:
In Jeremiah 32:27, You, God, state that 'I am the Lord, the God of all mankind. Is anything too hard for me?" Please today Lord, help (___) experience You in a new and might way. Help me remember that nothing is too difficult for You in my life and in (___)'s life. You have great things in store for each of us. I am going to praise You in advance for the work You are doing in their life now and in the future.

Life verse:
"I am the Lord, the God of all mankind. Is anything too hard for me?"
Jeremiah 32:27

Day 3
Feeling So Alone

Meditation Moment and Prayer:
Dear God, this is a time when (___) is going through something that seems so very horrendous. I feel like I'm the only one who has ever cried to you for this insurmountable request. I just can't talk about it with anyone due to the embarrassment or lack of understanding. I simply feel so alone right now. Please give me comfort in knowing that You are always with me. Remind me that there have been others who have experienced this type of pain. Please show me today that I am not alone.

> Even when the entire situation seems bleak,
> **God is the Alpha and the Omega**
> **The Beginning and the End.**
> Remember and trust this truth always.

There are numerous examples of prodigals in the Bible and in real life that can bring you encouragement during this difficult time in your prodigal's life. Let's explore a few of these stories in order to gain some valuable insight.

Jacob loved his son Joseph but Joseph's brothers were very jealous of that relationship. They planned on killing him, but decided instead to sell Joseph as a slave. What the brothers did in a jealous rage, God used to save their entire family and an entire nation. Jacob was told by his other sons that Joseph had been killed by a wild beast. Jacob mourned this loss for years while God continued to work in Joseph's life in ways that only He could ordain.

(We will discuss Joseph's story in Genesis 37 in more detail on a later day.)

Another example of a parent feeling totally alone is found in the story of heartbroken Jarius. His daughter hadn't turned her back on her faith but she had become gravely ill. Jarius was trying to find Jesus to ask for his help in healing his daughter. But as he was getting closer to the Master, "messengers arrived from the home of Jarius, the leader of the synagogue. They told him, 'Your daughter is dead. There's no use troubling the Teacher now.' (I can only imagine how alone he felt at that moment.) But Jesus overheard them and said to Jarius, 'Don't be afraid, just have faith.' Then Jesus stopped the crowd and wouldn't let anyone go with him except Peter, James, and John (the brother of James). When they came to the home of the synagogue leader, Jesus saw much commotion and weeping and wailing. He went inside and asked, 'Why all this commotion and weeping? The child isn't dead; she's only asleep.' The crowd laughed at him. He made them all leave, and he took the girl's father and mother and his three disciples into the room where the girl was lying. Holding her hand, he said to her, "Talitha Koum," which means "Little girl, get up!" And the girl, who was twelve years old, immediately stood up and walked around! They were overwhelmed and totally amazed." Mark 5:35-42.

Both of these fathers had to be beside themselves. They were beyond grieving. They were seeking God's intervention as quickly as possible. I'm sure they must have been thinking: "This can't be happening!" How alone they must have felt in those moments of desperation.

**Remember this:
No matter what the situation...
YOU ARE NOT ALONE.
God is in control and His timing is always perfect!!**

Prayer for the prodigal:
Lord today I pray that in my loneliness I remember that (___) must be feeling all alone as well. I pray that You would bring someone into his/her life who will show them Your grace and Your mercy and befriend them. Help me not focus so much on my loneliness but on Your control and timing. Use this loneliness to draw both of us closer to You and to each other.

Life verse:
"Turn to me and have mercy, for I am alone and in deep distress. My problems go from bad to worse. Oh, save me from them all!"
Psalm 25:16-17 (NTL)

Personal Prayers and Thoughts:

Day 4
Seeing the Bigger Picture

Meditation moment and prayer:
Lord, sometimes the choices are made for us. People can be mean, oppressive and downright evil. I ask that You remind me that You are able to and always do control each situation in our lives. I acknowledge that You see and know the whole story which is much bigger than I can see and understand right now.

Focus on this:
God is continually working His plan
which is always higher and broader
than we can imagine.

As we discovered yesterday, the story of Joseph in Genesis is a perfect example of how God is always working His plan. He alone can turn what is meant for evil into something really good.

When the brothers went back to their father, Jacob, they told him Joseph had been killed by a wild beast. Jacob had a proper burial and time of grieving which, I'm sure, lasted weeks, months and even all the years Joseph was gone. The anguish of losing a child is something that you can only fully understand when you have experienced it yourself. The gut wrenching grief flares up when you least expect it. I'm sure that Jacob constantly wished this was all just a bad joke or nightmare that would just go away. I'm sure he thought, "Maybe Joseph wasn't really killed." Maybe his brothers were mistaken and Joseph would just come walking in the door or across the field if Jacob looked hard enough. "Why Joseph??? Why now???" You can only imagine how he must have begged God many times. "Why not take me instead God?"

Even though your prodigal has not died, you are still grieving. Through that grief, you have felt and prayed the same. Why my beloved (___)? Why now?? God, what are you thinking? How can you use any of this for Your glory?

Let's NOT forget what God was up to in Joseph's life while Jacob was grieving! In the end of the story we are shown that Joseph didn't die but was actually used to save thousands of people with his unmatched leadership and planning skills. Throughout the land there was an enormous famine. After several years and many trials, Joseph was actually promoted to the equivalent of the Chief Financial Officer (CFO) of the entire nation and stored enough food away to feed thousands during the famine. Eventually even Joseph's brothers showed up to ask for aid. He immediately recognized them. Joseph showed mercy to his brothers because he knew this fact "God intended it all for good. " (As you can imagine, Joseph's father was thrilled to learn that Joseph was still alive and well.) You can find the full story in Genesis 37-50.

God always has THE full and complete picture in His sights. What we can see or know is only a small sliver of God's great plan. Trust Him to work in (___)'s life to complete His comprehensive plan in ways you may never imagine.

Prayer for the prodigal:
Father God, please turn (___)'s heart back to You. I trust You Lord to help shape their future to fit Your perfect plan. I know it may take more time than I think it should, so please help me remember this truth: You, Lord, are in control of all things.

Life verse:
"You intended to harm me but God intended it for good to accomplish what is now being done, the saving of many lives." Genesis 50:20

Personal Prayers and Thoughts:

Day 5
Keeping a Light On...What Does Light Really Do?

Meditation Moment and Prayer:
Dear Lord, as a light shines no matter what storms are blowing around it, please help me also be a shining beacon of hope for my prodigal. I don't know if I can be as silent as a glowing candle but teach me how to be the best example I can.

**Do not forget that:
God can work through even the tiniest of lights.**

Growing up in Central Illinois, there was often the threat of tornados coming across the open fields in the spring. As a precaution, my mother always kept candles and matches handy in case the power went out. This is a practice that I continue to this day. I have candles and matches in my home and office in the event the electricity goes out. Let's explore the reasons candlelight can make such a difference in a dark situation:
1) One small light can illuminate your path.
2) Light is never judgmental. It just shines.
3) It shows both the good and dangerous areas to walk.
4) It can protect you from the pitfalls that lie along the way.
5) A light's glow travels for miles penetrating the total darkness.
6) Light doesn't stop glowing just because something is standing in its way.

Light has only one job: to shine. That's how God created it in the beginning of time. Genesis 1:3 says "God said, 'Let there be light, and there was light.'"

Light illuminates the good things around us such as the sidewalk or the road in front of us. It also shows us dangers and pitfalls, such as all the toys on the living room floor, the potholes in the road or animals in a cave. The glow of one small candle can illuminate an entire room of darkness. You can see hundreds of feet in front of you with your headlights. Haven't you seen the glow in the sky on the pitch black night from a large city that is far away?

Luke 11:33 tells us "No one lights a lamp and puts it on a place where it will be hidden or under a bowl. Instead he puts it on the stand so that those who come in may see the light."

Make sure the light of your faith isn't hidden when you are communicating with your prodigal. Keep shining His love through your conversations and other forms of communication.

Prayer for the prodigal:
Lord, please show me ways to be a consistent light in this dark world so (___) and others will see You. I also pray (___) and their actions that are not pleasing to You will be exposed by the light of Your Word. Please help them see the truth about You and Your unfailing love for them through my consistent light of Your love.

Life verse:
"No one lights a lamp and puts it on a place where it will be hidden or under a bowl. Instead he puts it on the stand so that those who come in may see the light." Luke 11:33

Day 6
Silence Can Be Effective

Meditation moment and prayer:
Lord, You have commanded me to be a light in the darkness so people including (___) can see You shine through my life. But the thought of being a **SILENT** light is so foreign to me. Didn't you make us human to be able to share experiences and give guidance verbally? Help me to understand better this part of the light's role and be more like You Christ. Today help me be a steady but silent beacon shining for You Lord.

Remember this:
Light is silent.

Yes, lights are actually silent. They don't yell out instructions or constantly badger when someone is not walking the best route. You will never hear a porch light tell you, "Sorry I'm too tired or I'm just plain discouraged because no one has walked up the sidewalk lately." Nor will you hear a candle talk about extinguishing itself because "its feelings got hurt or it just didn't feel good today." Lights shine no matter what's going on around them. If there is a torrent of rain or violent winds, as long as the light has a power source, it will continue to shine.

Repeatedly in Scripture, Jesus instructs the people He had just healed or touched to go away in silence. In Mark 5:43 after Jesus had raised Jarius' daughter from the dead, "He gave strict orders not to let anyone know about this, and he told them to give her something to eat. In Mark 3:12 after casting out demons, Jesus again "gave them strict orders not to tell who He was."

Silence is a very powerful tool. It can allow for personal choices to be made without using a threatening tone. When my kids were preteens, I made a conscious decision to not escalate to their "pitch" when they got angry. I would purposefully whisper a response when one of them would yell or shout in anger and frustration. It worked every time because:
1) My whisper would catch their attention quicker than my yelling. It usually caught them off guard.
2) It forced them to stop and actually listen because it was so quiet.
3) It also helped me control my temper and frustration with the situation.

When you choose to be a light, silence is really the only option. So often we want to focus on changing the situation with our words instead of our actions and love. This usually leads to verbal arguments where very little is accomplished. A candle or light bulb cannot speak no matter what is happening in front of it. The light source dispels the darkness without subtle reminders of past hurts, open complaints about the current situation or gentle jabs of its own opinions. It simply lights the way.

Prayer for the prodigal:
Father of Lights, remind me moment by moment that silence may be best right now for my prodigal to see more of you. Forgive my condemning spirit toward (___). Help me silently offer praise for him/her. As Psalm 69:5-6 says "You know my folly, oh God, my guilt is not hidden from you. May those who hope in You not be

disgraced because of me, Lord, the Lord Almighty. May those who seek You not be put to shame because of me, God of Israel. "

Life verse:
"A gentle answer turns away wrath, but a harsh word stirs up anger."
Proverbs 15:1

Personal Prayers and Thoughts:

Day 7
Persistent Pestering

Meditation moment and prayer:
Lord, I continually fight the urge to be a nag. I want my voice and opinions to be heard but I realize now that if I'm truly to be a light for You, I must practice being silent. Help me remember that I can be a persistent praying pest to You instead of nagging to those around me. Give me a reminder that when I am tempted to 'nag', I can bug You with my prayers instead, just as the widow did to the judge.

**Remember this:
ALWAYS PRAY AND NEVER GIVE UP.**

A light that is left on can actually be both a benefit and a nuisance. We live in a fairly dark neighborhood. There are no street lights. Many of the homes, including ours, have lights that shine on them through the night. It's very beautiful as you drive down our street and see the lovely brick and stone homes lit at night. The true purposes of the lights are to give light if you arrive at the house after dark and to try to deter intruders from breaking in.

However, one of outside lights actually shines all night in through the glass in our front door. I am a very light sleeper and that light actually wakes me up throughout the night with its persistent shining. To me it's a pest. But to our home it adds beauty and protection.

The parable of the pestering widow is a very short but powerful one, which gives us continued hope that "the prayers of a righteous man/woman accomplish much." James 5:16.

"Then Jesus told his disciples a parable to show them that they should always prayer and never give up. He said: 'In a certain town there was a judge who neither feared God nor cared about men. And there was a widow in that town who kept coming to him with a plea. 'Grant me justice against my adversary.' For some time he refused. But finally he said to himself, 'Even though I don't fear God or care about men, yet this widow keeps bothering me. I will see that she gets justice so that she won't eventually wear me out with her coming!'
And the Lord said, 'Listen to what the unjust judge says. And will not God bring about justice for His chosen ones, who cry out to Him day and night? Will He keep putting them off? I tell you, He will see that they get justice and quickly." Luke 18:1-8

As you pray remember that His timing is not our own. His ways are higher than our thoughts and ways. Become the prayer pest. Keep asking, seeking and knocking. He will answer you. Luke 11:9 reminds us of this: "So I say to you, ask, and it will be given to you; seek, and you will find; knock and it will be opened to you."

When I was an 18 year old freshman in college, I collapsed one day in my dorm room from a debilitating headache. My parents rushed me to the hospital. I was admitted and given a battery of tests, including several hours of a CT scan of my brain. The doctors found the outline of a tumor on the lower part of my brain behind my right ear. As you can only imagine, my parents were very worried and fearful of what the diagnosis could be. The doctors wanted to do one more test the following day involving a dye injection to determine the exact size, dimensions, and location of the tumor before they made a final diagnosis and treatment plan. After my parents left the hospital that evening before this final test was to be performed, I started praying fervently. Even as an 18-year-old, I only wanted God's will for my life and this situation. I had nowhere else to turn. So I prayed. All night long I cried out to God asking for His peace and will to be done through all of this experience.

About 5:30 in the morning, the doctor came into my room. (I was scheduled to go for this test/procedure about 7 AM.). The doctor pulled a chair up beside my bed. He wanted me to know that they had reviewed the results from the previous day's CT scan. He determined that the tumor was no longer there!!! He repeated the news. The tumor they had seen on earlier reports was gone!!! He couldn't explain what had happened. But I immediately explained to him that God took it away!! I told him I had prayed all night and He had shown mercy to my situation. God is good!!

Press in…
Because God is faithful,
ALWAYS PRAY AND NEVER GIVE UP.

Prayer for your prodigal:
Lord in the coming days remind me to press in to You. Thank you for Your faithfulness throughout (___)'s life. You have provided before and I know You will do it again for (___). Today show me ways to specifically pray for (___). I acknowledge that You are creator of Heaven

and earth and You are still in the miracle working business. Help me live, pray, and think expectantly as You continue to do a work daily.

Life verse:
"And will not God bring about justice for His chosen ones, who cry out to Him day and night? Will He keep putting them off? I tell you, He will see that they get justice and quickly." Luke 18:7-8

Personal Prayers and Thoughts:

**Day 8
No Power...No light**

Meditation moment and prayer:
Lord right now, I feel so powerless in the current circumstances. I can personally do no more to change or help the situation with (___). Give me a new sense of power through your Holy Spirit to let your light shine through me. Forgive me as I always try to do things in my own strength. Help me learn to become more dependent on You.

**Do not forget:
When there is no power, there is no light.**

Let's talk about power sources for a few minutes. There are several sources of power that can illuminate paths: The flame that lights the candle, batteries in a flashlight or the electric current that lights the light bulb. But there is only ONE power source that can illuminate the path of a prodigal through our light: Jesus. In Matthew 5:14 & 16, Jesus says "You are the light of the world. The city on a hill cannot be hidden. Let your light shine before men in such a way that they may see your good works, and glorify your Father who is in heaven."

One time as a child I remember a very stormy night. The electricity flickered several times that evening causing the lights in the house to blink on and off. Finally when the lights came back on they were really dim and yellowish-brown looking. Each light gave off an eerie dim glow. My Dad called it a "brown out". That is when the flow of electricity from the power source to the house was diminished but not completely turned off. In brown out conditions, household appliances that run on electricity do not run at full capacity. The lights cast an ominous golden hue. The refrigerator kept kicking on and off which could have damaged the unit. So we had to unplug all the major appliances to protect them from this lack of power because they weren't getting all they needed to run efficiently.

When you and I try to be a bright light on our own, we often end up being in "brown out mode" with just barely enough energy to make a small glow. The results tend to be the same every time we try to help our prodigal; even it's for the 5th, 12th or 15th time we try to help. We end up drained of all our own energy and frustrated because our personal power source cannot sustain our efforts.

Our resource has to be Jesus Christ through the power of the Holy Spirit to carry us in times where we have no more answers, when our energy is totally drained or we feel as if we just cannot do it anymore. Allow the Holy Spirit to be your source of strength and fill you with everything you need. Praying God's word is one way the Holy Spirit can reenergize and empower us. Here are some examples of scripture prayers you can use regularly:

Romans 15:13 Paul says "May the God of hope fill you with all peace as you trust in Him, so that you may overflow with hope by the power of the Holy Spirit."

Isaiah 40:29-31 "He (The Lord) gives strength to the weary, and to him who lacks might He increases power. Though youths grow weary and tired, and vigorous young ones stumble badly, yet those who wait for the

Lord will gain new strength; they will mount up with wings like eagles, they will run and not be tired, they will walk and not become weary.

Prayer for the prodigal:
Today Lord I pray You grant me the strength and power I need to be more than a dim reflection of You. During this time of exhaustion and frailty, I bow before You, acknowledging my weakness. Fill me Lord with all that I need to shine brilliantly with Your love. I want to mount up with wings like eagles instead of struggling through on my own power.

Life verse:
"He (The Lord) gives strength to the weary, and to him who lacks might He increases power. Though youths grow weary and tired, and vigorous young ones stumble badly, yet those who wait for the Lord will gain new strength; they will mount up with wings like eagles, they will run and not be tired, they will walk and not become weary." Isaiah 40:29-31

Personal Prayers and Thoughts:

Day 9
How long Lord?

Meditation moment and prayer:
Heavenly father, I know Your ways are perfect and that includes Your timing. But seriously Lord... how long do we have to wait to see Your work happening in (___)'s life? Help me to trust that You are in control moment by moment. Forgive me when I want to be "in charge" and forget to trust Your timing.

If you will only remember one thing right now, take courage in this one fact:

God's timing is not the same as ours.
His timing is always perfect.

Read it again:
God's timing is always perfect.

When my son was an infant he was very sick. I was feeding him baby formula through that first year which was very expensive and we were on an extremely tight budget at the time. When he was 11 months old, I had enough formula for about one more week. After praying about what to do and while we were at an appointment, I specifically asked the pediatrician if I could just go ahead and switch my son over to whole milk before he turned 12 months old. The doctor strongly suggested that I continue with the formula for at least one more month since this little one had been through so much illness in his short life.

The doctor happened to mention this to the nurse as she

came in the room to give me the final instructions of the visit. She said, "Did I ever give you the postcard for the free formula?" I responded, "No I'm not aware of a free formula program." She reached into a drawer and handed me a green postcard. She instructed me to fill it out and stick in the mail in order to get some free formula in a few weeks.

I was thrilled and decided to fill it out right then and mail it in the blue mail receptacle right outside their office. I figured I could finish the formula I had at home which would last a couple more days. Then I would switch him to whole milk and supplement that with the baby formula samples when they arrived. I was thanking God for this option and then went about my day without giving it any more thought.

The next morning, the door bell rang. UPS had dropped off a package…it was a FULL CASE of baby formula!! That was enough to last one full month!! This was over $200 worth of baby formula that was literally dropped at our doorstep. How in the world did it get processed and delivered soooo quickly?? I could not believe my eyes! God was SO faithful and His timing could not have been more perfect!

In times of crisis and confusion, which seems to happen on a regular basis with your prodigal, I challenge you to start giving the worry and the planning to God. Start believing that **HE IS ABLE**. You may not know what to expect from Him just yet but start by simply believing that He is able and His timing is always perfect. God is in control of time and space. When things don't look right to you at the moment…just believe this one fact: **HE IS ABLE.**

Prayer for the prodigal:
Father God, time seems to go so slowly. Please help me love (___) patiently. I am trusting You to continue to work daily/moment by moment in their life and in mine. I want to increase my faith today by saying aloud: "God, You are able. You are watching this situation. You know the best timing for everything. You are able."

Life verse:
"But do not forget this one thing, dear friends: with the Lord a day is like a thousand years, and a thousand years are like a day. The Lord is not slow in keeping His promise, as some understand slowness. He is patient with you, not wanting anyone to perish, but everyone to come to repentance." 2 Peter 3:8-9

Personal Prayers and Thoughts:

Day 10
Light Can Guard the Path
But It Can't Keep Us from Falling

Meditation moment and prayer:
God of grace, I have made blunders along the way with (___) as a parent and a friend. I ask Your forgiveness for my mistakes and I pray that (___) can also forgive those times when I failed. Thank You that You are able to use my mistakes for Your glory. I am trusting You to make both of us more like You through Your plan and through my errors. Help me begin shining Your light better and brighter than ever.

**Always remember:
God doesn't make mistakes.
Thankfully He can use our mistakes for His glory
and to make each of us more like Him.**

When my children were young, as a mother I constantly guided them. At first I kept them as safe as I could at all times. I was a stay at home mother so I could control the friends they hung out with and the activities they did. We used the baby swing or stroller to keep them "contained" but safe. Once the kids got into preschool and elementary school, I lost some of that control. Even though I taught at their schools, I could only be more aware of the surroundings rather than actually being able to control their interactions.

Once they were grown, I had to realize the children God gave me are gifts from Him, that I can influence for His glory for only a short time. My responsibilities have now changed. Since they are grown, I am now in a prayer warrior/friend/mentor role rather than in a full-fledged parenting role. God's purpose and design for our adult children and for any adult for that matter, may not be the same as the goals we may have set for them. We know and must trust that His purposes for them are only designed with their best interest in mind. God doesn't make mistakes. Thankfully He can use our mistakes for His glory and to make us grow more like Him. We have to trust in that simple fact.

Prayer for the prodigal:
Lord, as a light shows the path much more clearly, please help me remember that You have a plan for (___). It is a plan to make them all You want them to be. Help me show love to (___) even though this path they have taken is different than what I would have chosen. Help me trust that You can still use their mistakes to make them grow into Your likeness.

Life verse:
"I thank my God every time I remember you. I always pray with joy... being confident of this that He who began a good work in you will carry it on to completion until the day of Christ Jesus."
Philippians 1:3-6

Day 11
How Could This Heartache be God's Will?

Meditation moment and prayer:
Heavenly Father surely You are seeing all the bad stuff that's been happening. I can't imagine how You can allow all of this heartache to take place. Help me understand You in a more complete way even though my wisdom is so finite and limited.

>**Consider this:**
>**He sees all things.**
>**God is not blind to the things**
>**that are going on.**

No one can fully understand the scope of the purposes behind what happens in our lives. For all of us, this is a difficult truth to accept. In our day and time, we have so many research tools at our disposal – the Internet, books, TV, libraries, etc. With all of this information at our fingertips we often strive to fully control and understand things for ourselves: our lives, environment, circumstances and our surroundings, etc.

So often there are circumstances and situations that we simply cannot explain or understand. When we feel out of control in these situations, society can make us think that we have failed in some way. So why does God allow for certain things to happen: cancer in children, killings everywhere, divorce, addictions, death…?? "Why God?" we ask.

Thankfully, God is beyond our full understanding. This gives us reason to have faith. Faith is defined as something that is hoped for but not yet seen. God has a different perspective than we do: knowing this is where our faith in Him will give us peace in the midst of confusion. Honestly we will never have the full answers to all of these questions while we live on earth.

Let's take a look at the story of Job. God said these words about him in Job 1:8 "There is no one on earth like him (Job); he is blameless and upright, a man who fears God and shuns evil." When you read on in chapter 1, Satan actually challenged God about Job's hedge of protection. He thought Job would recant his faith in God if all his good 'stuff' was taken away. So God allowed Satan to touch Job's possessions but not Job's life. In doing this, God invited Satan to test Job and Satan took God up on the suggestion! Why would God do such a thing? What was the motivation behind that decision? Was it to see what Job was made of? Was it to give us an example of God's faithfulness after terrible trials?

Job's tragedy was incomprehensible and definitely raised questions that can't be answered even with today's best technology. But let's take a close look at Job's response to the tragedy in his life.

In less than one day (actually within a matter of a few hours), Job found out that all 10 of his children were killed, most of the servants and livestock were also dead and all of his possessions were burned or stolen!! Did he cry out "Why me God..?? Why my kids, Lord??"

No.

Actually this was Job's reply to all of this unspeakable

tragedy: "Then he (Job) fell to the ground in worship and said 'Naked I come from my mother's womb and naked I will depart. The Lord gave and the Lord has taken away. May the name of the Lord be praised.' **In all of this, Job did not sin by charging God with wrongdoing."** Job 1:20b-22

God had a bigger plan for Job's life. Through great anguish and sorrow, Job continued to praise God's name for all things: the good, the bad, the dreadful, and all the heartbreak. In all those things Job trusted that God was watching and that God was in control, even when nothing made sense. In the end, not only did Job regain his wealth and family but God is using his story today (several thousand years later) to give us hope in our darkest times. Job 42:10-17

Prayer for your prodigal:
Lord, I confess that I don't understand why You allow all of this heartache in my life right now. It seems to never end. But I want to trust you more that You really do see what is going on and that You are still in control of the situation in (___)'s life. Please give (___) faith in You to carry them through this difficult time and see You at work in their life.

Life verse:
"The Lord is my light and my salvation-whom shall I fear?
The Lord is the stronghold of my life-of whom shall I be afraid?
When evil men advance against me to devour my flesh, when my enemies and my foes attack me, they will stumble and fall.

Though an army besieges me, I will not fear.
Though war break out against me, even then will I be confident.
I am still confident of this: I will see the goodness of the Lord in the land of the living. Wait for the Lord; be strong and take heart and wait for the Lord."
Psalm 27:1-3 & 13-14.

Day 12
Blurry, Scuffed Up Old Sunglasses

Meditation moment and prayer:
Father God, I get so overwhelmed with the negative and all the tragedy. It's hard to see clearly. Lord, help me today keep my eyes on You and not on the world or things that are happening around me.

In Colossians 3, Paul encourages us to "Set your hearts on things above, where Christ is seated at the right hand of God. Set your mind on things above, not on earthly things."

> **Keep this in mind:**
> **Improve your focus by**
> **setting your heart and mind**
> **on the higher things of God.**

So often your prodigal is constantly on your mind. Where are they now? How are they doing? Why do they always want to do the same old things? There are always so many questions going on in your mind. Often you focus on all of the negative things about your prodigal which can breed resentment and anger. When "the resentment lens" begins to consume your thoughts and vision, it is like wearing a blurry, cuffed up pair of old sunglasses. You can still see things but they don't look clear. Your vision is clouded.

In Colossians 3, Paul encourages us to "Set your hearts of things above, where Christ is seated at the right hand of God. Set your mind on things above, not on earthly things." Paul is challenging you to check your heart.

Remember that: what your mind focuses on, your heart will embrace. Have you become negative and bitter by your thoughts toward your prodigal? Capture that. Let God help you grow beyond that negativity and take off those blurry glasses. Improve your focus by setting your heart and mind on higher, more eternal things. Focus your thoughts on God's overall purpose and God's ability to help you and your prodigal overcome.

Colossians 3:5-10 tells us what to **set aside**:
- Vs 5: "Put to death therefore, whatever belongs to your earthly nature: sexual immorality, impurity, lust, evil desires and greed, which is idolatry."
- Vs 8-9: " but now you must rid yourselves of all such things as these: anger, rage, malice, slander, and all filthy language from your lips. Do not lie to each other..."

Colossians 3:12-17 tells us what to **focus on** instead:
- Vs 12: "Therefore, as God's chosen people, holy and dearly loved, clothe yourselves with compassion, kindness, humility, gentleness and patience.
- Vs 13: "Bear with each other and forgive whatever grievances you may have against one another. Forgive as the Lord forgave you.
- Vs 14: "And over all these virtues put on love..."
- Vs 15: "Let the peace of Christ rule in your hearts... And be thankful."
- Vs 16: "Let the word of Christ dwell in you richly..."
- Vs 17: "And whatever you do, whether in word or deed, do it all in the name of the Lord Jesus, giving thanks to God the Father through Him. "

Colossians 3:23 and 4:2 sum up what we can personally strive for.
- Col 3:23 "Whatever you do, work at it with all your heart, as working for the Lord, not for men…"
- Col 4:2 "Devote yourselves to prayer, being watchful and thankful…"

Prayer for the prodigal:
God of grace and mercy, please help me take off the resentment filter I have been looking through, like a blurry, scuffed up pair of old sunglasses. I want to see (___) through Your eyes today. I ask that somehow (___) will be willing to forgive me for being so negative and focusing constantly on their problems and mistakes. Help me to be conscious of the times when I am not being positive or thinking on positive things. Help me follow what Colossians 3 is teaching me so that I will be a brighter light to (___) every time I talk to him/her.

Life verse:
"Devote yourselves to prayer, being watchful and thankful…"
Colossians 4:2

Personal Prayers and Thoughts:

Day 13
Shine Brighter Than Usual

Meditation moment and prayer:
Lord of heaven and earth, thank You for loving me enough to allow me to grow through this whole process. Give me eyes to see a new opportunity to shine my light for You. Perhaps there is someone else who needs light from the knowledge that I have learned through this experience. Guide me as I want to share Your light and love more.

Consider this:
God can use you in the life of
someone else's prodigal
to bring Himself glory.

Have you ever considered that God may have your prodigal in this place to use you for His glory? I would challenge you to be His light not only to your beloved prodigal but to those in a similar situation. Perhaps you could serve in a homeless shelter or minister to addicts in a rehab center. Maybe it's just simply being willing to get to know your prodigal's friends and show them the unconditional love of Christ.

Let's look at Jesus' example in Matthew 25:34-40. "Then the king will say to those on his right… For I was hungry and you gave me something to eat. I was thirsty and you gave me something to drink. I was a stranger and you invited me in. I needed clothes and you clothed me, I was sick and you looked after me, I was in prison and you came to visit me…Whatever you did for one of the least of these brothers of mine, you did for me. "

Several years ago while attending the local county fair; I was outside the small one seat ticket booth waiting to buy tickets for the carnival rides. As I reached in to pay for my tickets, I noticed the woman in the booth had a newborn baby wrapped in a large white t-shirt. I asked her about the baby whom she said was just about three weeks old. As I walked away (putting two and two together), my heart ached for this young mother and child. So I went back to the booth when she wasn't too busy and just talked to her. She told me she had no clothes for the little one and they were letting her work in the ticket booth because it was the only place on the midway that had air conditioning.

The next evening I decided to go back to the fair and drop off a few things as a surprise for the baby: some 'onesies', sleepers and diapers. The woman was speechless. She honestly didn't know what to say. At first she said, "No, thank you. I can't pay you for these." I just explained they were a free gift for the baby and I hoped she could use them. She broke into tears and was very grateful.

In actuality, the clothing and supplies were free to me. Several weeks before, our region had been devastated by two tornados on the same day! Our church had become a collection point for many of the donations that had poured into the region. Those donations were distributed as needed but there were many items left over. I simply got permission to use those supplies for this mother in need. Our church staff was more than willing to share these supplies with anyone who could use them.

By taking the time to notice that one young mother in need, this action ended up leading to a three year ministry project for carnival workers at the local county fair. I discovered they need simple things like underwear, socks, jeans, soap and shampoo. God allowed me to see a need that was easy for me to meet at that time and I was willing to follow His leading. Through that I was able to better understand how the life of carnival workers plays out and the struggles they face. I'm sure many of them are prodigals themselves.

We just never know the impact we can have when we touch someone in Jesus' name. So step out of your comfort zone and pray about ministry opportunities that God could bring your way. Help with a food pantry, a local clothing bank, or a homeless shelter. Take some time to actually get to know some of the patrons. Who are they? Where are they from? What interests do they have? Where is their family? Share some love by showing some interest in them. You will be amazed how God will help you grow through giving in this way. It will also give you a new perspective on how to pray for your prodigal and others.

Prayer for the prodigal:
Lord, you know where (___) is right now. Please bring into their life someone who loves You beyond measure and will be a bright light to them in the circumstance they're in today. And I pray that You will bless that person tremendously for shining Your light in the exact way that (___) needs it this week.

Life verse:
"Whatever you did for one of the least of these brothers of mine, you did for me." Matthew 25:40

Personal Prayers and Thoughts:

Day 14
Leave a Light on Even Through the Worst of the Storm

Meditation moment and prayer:
"Oh God, … We have no power to face this vast army that is attacking us. We do not know what to do, but our eyes are upon you." (2 Chronicles 20:12) God, it seems like the bad news just keeps coming. There's been another phone call or another disaster or another emergency. God, I don't know what to do right now. I don't know how to be the most effective light in this complete and total darkness. Please give me insight on what to do next.

> **This is what the LORD says to you:**
> **'Do not be afraid or discouraged**
> **because of this vast army.**
> **For the battle is not yours, but God's."**

The storm is raging and everything just seems to be falling apart with the situation. All of a sudden you get one more phone call or piece of news that is devastating. What do you do? Where do you turn? Are you willing to humble yourself enough to pray as King Jehoshaphat did: "I have no power against this vast army of God. I do not know what to do...But my eyes are on You."

Let's take a look at Jehoshaphat's situation and how God answered that humble prayer of panic. The story is found in 2 Chronicles 20.
- Vs 2-4 "Some people came and told Jehoshaphat, "A vast army is coming against you from Edom, from the other side of the Dead Sea…Alarmed, Jehoshaphat resolved to inquire of the LORD, and he proclaimed a fast for all Judah. The people of

Judah came together to seek help from the LORD; indeed, they came from every town in Judah to seek him."
- Vs 5-12 "Then Jehoshaphat stood up in the assembly...and said: "O LORD, the God of our ancestors, are You not the God who is in heaven? You rule over all the kingdoms of the nations. Power and might are in Your hand, and no one can withstand You. Our God, did You not drive out the inhabitants of this land before Your people Israel and give it forever to the descendants of Abraham Your friend? They have lived in it and have built in it a sanctuary for Your Name, saying, 'If calamity comes upon us, whether the sword of judgment, or plague or famine, we will stand in Your presence before this temple that bears Your Name and will cry out to You in our distress, and You will hear us and save us.' But now here are men from Ammon, Moab and Mount Seir, whose territory You would not allow Israel to invade when they came from Egypt; so they turned away from them and did not destroy them...Our God, will You not judge them? For we have no power to face this vast army that is attacking us. We do not know what to do, but our eyes are on You."
- Vs 15b "...This is what the LORD says to you: **'Do not be afraid or discouraged because of this vast army. For the battle is not yours, but God's."**
- Vs 17-18 "You will not have to fight this battle. Take up your positions; stand firm and see the deliverance the LORD will give you, Judah and Jerusalem. **Do not be afraid; do not be discouraged.** Go out to face them tomorrow, and the LORD will be with you. 'Jehoshaphat bowed

down with his face to the ground, and all the people of Judah and Jerusalem fell down in worship before the LORD."
- Vs 20-22 "Early in the morning they left for the Desert of Tekoa. As they set out, Jehoshaphat stood and said, "Listen to me, Judah and people of Jerusalem! **Have faith in the LORD your God and you will be upheld**; have faith in his prophets and you will be successful." After consulting the people, Jehoshaphat appointed men to sing to the LORD and to praise Him for the splendor of His holiness as they went out at the head of the army, saying: "Give thanks to the LORD, for His love endures forever." As they began to sing and praise, the LORD set ambushes against the men of Ammon and Moab and Mount Seir who were invading Judah, and they were defeated."
- Vs 24-25 "When the men of Judah came to the place that overlooks the desert and looked toward the vast army, they saw only dead bodies lying on the ground; no one had escaped. So Jehoshaphat and his men went to carry off their plunder, and they found among them a great amount of equipment and clothing and also articles of value — more than they could take away. There was so much plunder that it took three days to collect it."

God honors the panic strickened prayer. We also must follow His commands as part of the plan. Jehoshaphat did not allow the panic and fear to dampen his light. He immediately turned to God. Jehoshaphat prayed and the people prayed. Then they listened and followed the command.

I'm sure that everyone was confused when they were told to just start singing as they headed into battle instead of fighting. That strategy made absolutely no sense to the human mind. However they were willing to do exactly as they were told to do. Even though, it didn't make sense. And God honored their faithfulness by providing all they needed and more in the battle.

So I want to repeat this same word for you now:

When things seem to be spiraling out of control and are really scary...
**"Do not be afraid or discouraged
because of this vast army.
For the battle is not yours, but God's."**

Prayer for the prodigal:
God of all power and might, I give you this "vast army" and incredibly overwhelming situation. I do not know where to turn. But I am trusting You to intervene in (___)'s life in a way that only You can. I pray for anyone who comes in contact with (___) today --please give them wisdom and guidance. Please touch each of their lives as they work with (___) right now. Show me what to pray and how to 'fight' even if it just involves singing and praising You.

Life verse:
"Do not be afraid or discouraged because of this vast army. For the battle is not yours, but God's."
 2 Chronicles 20:15b

Personal Prayers and Thoughts:

Day 15
Always Expect Greatness

Meditation moment and prayer:
Today, Lord God, as the Psalmist did in
Psalm 103:1-5, I will "Praise the Lord, O my soul, all my inmost being, praise His holy name. Praise the Lord, O my soul, and forget not His benefits – who forgives all your sins and heals all your diseases, who redeems your life from the pit and crowns you with love and compassion, who satisfies your desires with good things so that your youth is renewed like the eagles." Forgive me when I forget to praise You and I forget to expect great things from You, Lord. Help me focus on Your ability to work in this situation rather than all the upsetting things going on.

Focus on this:
God works in the most unusual ways—
Don't limit Him!!

As you learned yesterday about Jehoshaphat's huge battle, you also need to understand that even though the plan was so unusual, God showed up. And great things happened. We have to be trusting in the same thing...that God is working and He will finish that good work.

Several years ago my husband and I were hit with a huge financial debt unexpectedly. We weren't sure where to turn. We did not have the money to cover the debt in the time frame given. That is when God showed me Jehoshaphat's story in 2 Chronicles 20. The night we got word of this debt repayment responsibility I cried to the

Lord in fear and panic just as Jehoshaphat had done. I prayed "We have no power to face this vast army that is attacking us. We do not know what to do, but our eyes are upon You."

I ended up on my knees praying, fasting and crying to God for one week. Over that time, miraculously, God allowed for several large checks to come in from my husband's business earlier than we were expecting. Guess what? The amount of those unexpected checks was EXACTLY the amount we needed to cover the debt repayment responsibility!!! God is working and He will finish that good work. We just have to fully trust Him and His timing.

Once again, Jeremiah 32:27 rings true: "I am the Lord, the God of all mankind. Is anything too hard to me?" Don't limit God with your small frame of reference. Go to Him expectantly…Nothing is too hard for Him!!

Prayer for the Prodigal:
God of all mankind, thank You for being concerned about both the major issues and the seemingly small details of our lives. Help both (___) and I realize today that You are working out details that we can't imagine. I trust You though this 'vast army that is attacking'. Thank you that this battle is not mine but You have it all in control. I trust You with (___)'s life and situation today even though I can't imagine how it's all going to work out.

Life verse:
"I am the Lord, the God of all mankind. Is anything too hard for me?"
Jeremiah 32:27

Day 16
A Light Shines with Confidence

Meditation moment and prayer:
Lord God of all creation, thank You for giving me Your Word as encouragement and strength. Help me continue to trust You with more confidence and faith than ever before. Help me stand firm in Psalm 27:13-14 "I am still confident of this: I will see the goodness of the Lord in the land of the living. Wait for the Lord; be strong and take heart and wait for the Lord."

> **Do not forget this:**
> **We have never been promised**
> **an easy path through life.**
> **But we have been promised**
> **the strength needed to persevere.**

One day when my children were really young, probably ages 7 & 5, I overheard them talking about something that was upsetting my 5-year-old son. Without hesitation, his "older, wiser" 7-year-old sister blurts out, "Well, life just isn't fair." I almost laughed out loud as I thought of the irony of that instruction. Obviously she had heard that from her mother several times!! Ha ha!! She was right. We have never been promised an easy path through life. But we have been promised the strength needed to persevere.

Through all of my dark discouraging days, Psalm 34:1 has become my battle cry: "I **WILL** praise the Lord no matters what happens. I will **constantly** speak of His glories and grace." It is so important to make a conscious effort to stay positive through all the tough, exhausting times. This is not an easy thing to do. Unfortunately life isn't fair.

My mother fought breast cancer and colon cancer for 27 years of her 75 year life. She had many years of remission but also numerous trips to a doctor's office where she and my Dad were given devastating news, the cancer had come back. Through it all: their fears, emotional highs and lows, the months and months of chemo and radiation, etc. she continued to praise God for His enduring love and faithfulness. Her testimony through all of that long battle was always to shine her light confidently. She knew WHO her power source came from and her light was always glowing with God's goodness and provision. Does that mean every day was perfect for her? ABSOLUTELY NOT. Does that mean life was 'fair' to her? ABSOLUTELY NOT. But it does mean my Mom CHOSE to focus on the goodness of God in the midst of her pain and misery. You can too.

Prayer for the prodigal and life verse:
Father, help me praise You no matter what happens. Help me constantly speak of Your glories and grace even though things are going crazy with (___) and my world in general right now. I want to choose to praise You. "I will bless the Lord at all times. His praise shall continually be in my mouth."
 Psalm 34:1

Day 17
Avoid Being the Flashing Yellow Light

Meditation moment and prayer:
Today Lord, help me again focus on what I say and how I say it. Remind me today that You are in control and I don't have to try to figure out all of the details and resolutions. I simply have to trust You to take care of it all in Your timing.

> **Remember this:**
> **Learn to become FULLY dependent on God**
> **rather than just using Him as your crutch.**

A Traffic light consists of three different colors on purpose. Each of those different colors represent some type of communication, as you know. In our society, a green light typically means that all is clear. It should be safe for you to go forward with your plans or travels. The yellow light means slow down and proceed with caution. Be prepared to dramatically adjust your route or plans. Likewise, the red light tells us to stop. Do not go forward. Put your plans on hold for the time being or you could encounter serious consequences.

Being the oldest of four girls, I have always been an extreme caregiver. I love helping others and want to make sure everyone is comfortable and happy. As a result, I have always privately had a "plan B" all figured out in my head for most situations I might encounter. Subconsciously, my life was controlled by a constant

yellow flashing light. I always had "what-if" scenarios going through my mind:
1) What would we do if the car broke down?
2) What would we do if my husband lost his job?
3) How would we deal with a serious illness, cancer, etc?

This constant sense of worry and planning actually caused me to focus on all the negative that was going on (or could go on) in life. Outwardly I considered myself a very positive person. But in reality, God has shown me that I was being completely negative as I was always waiting for "the wreck to happen" or "the bottom to drop out" in my life.

It's easy to get that way with your prodigal...constantly worrying where/when/how the next catastrophe will happen. Let's look at a rather unlikely story in God's Word that will help us keep our perspective more positive.

In Mark 6:30-38 Mark tells us: "The apostles gathered around Jesus and reported to him all they had done and taught. Then, because so many people were coming and going that they did not even have a chance to eat, he said to them, 'Come with me by yourselves to a quiet place and get some rest.'

"So they went away by themselves in a boat to a solitary place. But many who saw them leaving recognized them and ran on foot from all the towns and got there ahead of them. When Jesus landed and saw a large crowd, he had compassion on them, because they were like sheep without a shepherd. So he began teaching them many things.

"By this time it was late in the day, so his disciples came to him. 'This is a remote place,' they said, 'and it's already very late. Send the people away so they can go to the surrounding countryside and villages and buy themselves something to eat.' But he answered, 'You give them something to eat.' They said to him, 'That would take eight months of a man's wages! Are we to go and spend that much on bread and give it to them to eat?'"

In other words, the disciples were probably saying...we cannot afford to do this...this is too big of a problem for us...You want us to do WHAT??!!!!! I'm sure the disciples had been talking among themselves before they went to Jesus. I'm starving...Man, it's getting so late... What are we going to do with all of these people?!?!? Panic may have been setting in as they were trying to figure out a "plan B."

Let's see how Jesus responds to their "plan B."
Mark 6:38-44 goes on with the rest of the story. "'How many loaves do you have?' he asked. 'Go and see.' When they found out, they said, 'Five --- and two fish.' Then Jesus directed them to have all the people sit down in groups on the green grass. So they sat down in groups of hundreds and fifties. Taking the five loaves and the two fish and looking up to heaven, he gave thanks and broke the loaves. Then he gave them to his disciples to set before the people. He also divided the two fish among them all. They all ate and were satisfied, and the disciples picked up twelve basketfuls of broken pieces and fish. The number of men who had eaten was five thousand."

(That number doesn't include the women and children! So the crowd was at least 10,000!!)

Just like the disciples in this example, I would always be praising God and verbally saying I was trusting Him. In reality I was only leaning on God rather than being fully dependent on Him. It was like I was using God as my crutch rather than my wheelchair. With crutches, you only have to lean on them while you move under your own power. In a wheelchair you HAVE to fully depend on the chair to support you and help you get to where you need to go. I genuinely believed I could formulate a plan to take care of any and every situation that could arise. What a pride-filled existence. I was actually cheating myself from allowing God to show up and work in all the situations. Thankfully Jesus overruled the disciples' ideas. He once again showed Himself strong through the miracles that happened that day.

Prayer for the Prodigal:
Father God, forgive me for always trying to second guess or jump ahead of your plans. I want to fully trust You with (___). Once again, continue to remind me that You are working miracles even when the current situation doesn't make any sense. Guard me from being the yellow flashing light all the time -- looking for possible problems. Help me recognize You are working in (___)'s life today in particular.

Life verse:
"Oh taste and see the Lord is good, how blessed is the man who takes refuge in Him!" Psalms 34:8

Day 18
Focus like Camera Flash

Meditation moment and prayer:
Father God so often my focus is on all the problems and heartache we have gone through with (___). Please forgive me for this negative attitude and point of view. Help me concentrate today on only praising You for (___). So often I get too focused on all the bad decisions and heartache. Help me throughout today to consciously remember to praise You for their life. Give me a renewed focus on the positive at least for today. Like the light of a camera flash, give me snapshots of positive attributes of and pleasant memories with (___).

> **Never forget:**
> **We are each fearfully and**
> **wonderfully made in His image.**

Generally, cameras are used to help document and remember pleasant experiences. We have the camera out and the flash going when we are traveling to fun places or during happy times with family and friends. Rarely do we snap pictures during sad or discouraging times. I never take a camera to a funeral, snap pictures of someone who is throwing up in the bathroom or writhing in pain on their hospital bed. Those are memories we just don't want to hold on to.

On the other hand, a security camera is put in place to record problems. Security camera footage is never reviewed to see how cute the child is or what the adorable little puppy has been up to. Security camera footage is viewed only when there has been a problem: a robbery, a shooting, etc. Why is it then that as each day passes it's so easy to remember only the trouble that your prodigal has gotten into? Or all the headache you have had to endure? It's like we are constantly reviewing security camera footage to remind us of all the disappointments rather than those photos of happier times.

My challenge to you is to purposefully focus your thoughts on the positive attributes of your prodigal throughout today. Do not let those negative, destructive memories dominate your thoughts today. Take those thoughts captive. Refuse to harbor the hurts for at least this one day. As one of those bad pictures from life's album comes to your mind, immediately replace it with one from a happier time. Make a list of your prodigal's attributes. This is also an acknowledgement to God that you realize (___) is fearfully and wonderfully made.

Prayer for the Prodigal:
Lord God, Creator of all life, thank you for (___). No matter how much heartache and grief has happened, (___) is Your creation and he/she is fearfully and wonderfully made. Throughout today, Lord, please bring to my mind memories of happy times we have had together. Help me to not focus on the disappointments and hurt all day. Help me to be the bright flash of the camera that is focused on enjoyable subjects rather than the security camera which is only taking video to find fault. Please give (___) a positive uplifting day today as well. Help him/her somehow see You are the provider of all things in his/her life.

Life verse:
"I praise You because I am fearfully and wonderfully made; Your works are wonderful, I know that full well." Psalm 139:14.

Personal Prayers and Thoughts:

Day 19

Shine Your Light Brightly

Meditation moment and prayer:
Lord God, Creator of all light, help me understand better what type of light you want me to be. Help me to always shine Your reflection brightly in dark situations and temper my light so all can see You better if things get cloudy or foggy.

**Think on this:
God calls us to be HIS light constantly.**

Recently there was a study on the effectiveness of headlights. There are several types of headlamps for automobiles: regular lights, high beams, fog lamps, etc. Each headlight in a car has a specific purpose:
1) Low beams are used to help you see the road more clearly and be seen by other drivers on the road;
2) High beams are used for seeing longer distances on darker nights;
3) Fog lamps are used to shine on the pavement lower so the light is not too obscured by the fog.
4) New LED headlights are used to shine further and brighter than the normal headlamps.

Certain situations call for the use of each of these various lights. As you move through different driving conditions, these lights are used to assist at the proper time.

When dealing with your prodigal, different types of "light" may also be needed in certain situations to make situations easier to deal with. God calls us to be HIS light constantly. So we need to continue to burn the headlights day or night but utilize some of the other lights that He has given us when the need arises, i.e., to be a brighter light when the truth in love needs to be spoken; to be a more indirect light when you aren't communicating directly with your prodigal.

Many years ago when I was a student at the University of Kentucky, there was a guy who was very faithful at 'sharing God's message' every single day outside in front of the student center. He was there rain or shine, warm or cold, day and night. (In fact I'm not sure when he slept.) This guy would continuously yell at people passing by shouting "You are a sinner." "You need to repent." "You need Jesus." Unfortunately his light was so bright that it was basically blinding for the people who were passing by. He was using condemnation and harsh words as a form of "ministry".

Even though he was "shining his light" for God so intensely, it was actually offensive to most of us. It was as if he was a police car with all of its flashing red, white and blue lights or like a strobe light blinding the message. You know what I mean, when you come upon a cop with all his lights blazing in the pitch dark night. It's almost overwhelming because it's so bright.

I don't believe this is the type of light that Jesus asks us to be in all situations. Jesus went to the sinners and got to know them. He ate with them, talked with them, and understood their life. He was always showing them love even through confrontation. This is the kind of light that we need to be. Someone who shines God's love in the midst of the trials while getting to know people one-on-

one like the running lights on your vehicle. They are on constantly, not too bright or too dim...just constant.

Prayer for the prodigal:
Lord teach me to be the right kind of light for You in each specific situation. I pray that (__) will see the exact light shining from my life that he/she needs right now in this moment. No matter what is going on between us, remind me not to be a critical, glaring light but to be one that draws attention to You.

Life verse:
"You are the light of the world. A city set on a hill cannot be hidden; nor does anyone light a lamp and put it under a basket, but they put it on a stand and it gives light to everyone in the house."
Matthew 5:14-15

Personal Prayers and Thoughts:

Day 20
When it seems the Darkest, Don't Forget to Just Look...

Meditation moment and prayer:
Lord God, sometimes I get so discouraged as I have been focusing on all the complexities of the situation. I feel like I'm beating my head against the wall constantly trying to be a positive light in the darkness. Sometime it would be nice to just take a break and rest from the worries and frustrations. Help me continually remember to look away from the negative and look to You and Your provisions that may be right in front of me. Help me remember that You are my light in this darkness. I can only reflect the light that I get from You.

**Seriously consider that:
God is calling you to find rest in Him.**

We were recently on a cruise to Alaska. The cruise ship was enormous (about 1,033 feet long and 121 feet wide). It was obviously very hard to miss as we were sailing up the Inside Passage along the Canadian coastline. As we left the port of Ketchikan, Alaska, I was standing on our balcony watching the beautiful scenery along the shoreline when I noticed a bird flying right alongside the ship. It was not a large bird. It looked to be about the size of a seagull. As the ship was gaining speed, amazingly this bird kept up. It was hard for me to judge the distance but it was close enough to the ship for me to watch him without binoculars.

After miles and miles of flying and with land several miles away, the bird kept flapping his wings. I thought how exhausted that bird must be getting! Why doesn't that bird just turn his head? He could literally have found complete rest on the HUGE ship that was only a few feet away. Instead, after miles and miles, the bird just suddenly turned around and started flying back toward Ketchikan.

I couldn't help but wonder how often we do the same thing. We are flapping and flapping through life over the ocean of worry and trials getting more and more exhausted as we go. We don't think to look next to us at the blinding light of this enormous ship of rest called Jesus. Instead we just keep looking down at the water and the waves underneath us. Panic sets in and we turn back toward whatever 'security' we remember, i.e. fret, worry, gossiping to others about how terrible things are, etc. There are lights everywhere and yet we are too distracted by our fret and worry to realize we are missing some much needed rest and security.

Matthew 14:22-33 tells us about a time when Jesus actually demonstrated that He was the place of rest on rough seas. "Immediately Jesus made the disciples get into the boat and go on ahead of him to the other side while he dismissed the crowd... When evening came...the boat was a considerable distance from land, buffeted by the waves because the wind was against it. During the fourth watch of the night Jesus went out to them, walking on the water. When the disciples saw him walking on the lake, they were terrified. 'It's a ghost,' they said and cried out in fear. But Jesus immediately said to them: 'Take courage!!! It is I. Do not be afraid.' 'Lord if it's you,' Peter replied, 'tell me to come to you on the water.'

'Come.' Jesus said. Then Peter got down out of the boat, walked on the water and came toward Jesus. But when he saw the wind, he was afraid and beginning to sink, he cried out, 'Lord, save me!'

"Immediately, Jesus reached out his hand and caught him. 'You of little faith,' he said, 'why did you doubt?' And when they climbed into the boat the wind died down. Then those who were in the boat worshiped by saying 'Truly you are the son of God!'"

How can you be the light God is calling you to be if you are completely exhausted, terrified and focused on the wind and the waves? God is calling you to take rest in Him. But He is not going to force you to rest. Just as the captain of the cruise ship did not take the time to turn the ship right into the bird's path in order to force rest upon the bird, you are given a choice. Jesus says he 'gently knocks at the door and waits for our answer." (Revelation 3:20)

Where is your focus? Are you exhausted? Take God at His word. Take courage. Be honest with yourself and God. Trust Him to work out the situation.

Prayer for the prodigal:
Heavenly Father, I do acknowledge that You are God over all the winds and the waves both physically and metaphorically. I am exhausted with worry and fear. I lay all these worries and fears for my prodigal at your feet today. I completely trust (___) into Your care this hour. Remind me today, moment by moment, that You can take care of (___) much better than I can and that You

are working constantly in their life. I praise You in advance for all that You are doing.

Life verse:
"Behold, I stand at the door and knock; if anyone hears my voice and opens the door, I will come into him..." Revelation 3:20.

Day 21
Praise for Protection

Meditation moment and prayer:
Lord one of my biggest fears is that (___) will get hurt or worse, die. When people are young there is usually someone there to protect them. (___) is grown now and I cannot physically protect them. So I am going to consciously praise You for protection. Thank You that You have a watchful eye. Even though (___) makes bad and sometimes dangerous choices, You can protect them. In confessing this fear to You, help me continue to focus on praising You instead of focusing on the fear.

**A challenge for you today:
Expect protection and an awakening.**

In 1 Samuel, we read where King Saul had been given word that David was the heir apparent king (even though Saul was still reigning king). Saul was not pleased with this news so he and his army chased David and his men all over the place. David was literally running for his life for about 20 years. I am sure David wondered why…why was he being chased like a common criminal when he had been such a man of God? I honestly can't tell you all of the reasons but there is part of this story that demonstrates God's sovereign protection very clearly.

In 1 Samuel 24:2. "So Saul took three thousand chosen men from all of Israel and set out to look for David…. He came to the sheep's pen along the way; a cave was there, and Saul went in to relieve himself. (He went to the bathroom.)… David and his men were far back in the cave….Then David crept up unnoticed and cut off a corner of Saul's robe."

Basically David (the pursued) caught Saul (the pursuer) with "his pants down", literally!!! David and his men could have easily killed Saul right then and there. However, let's read the rest of the story…

"Afterward David was conscious-stricken for having cut off a corner of King Saul's robe. He said to his men, 'The Lord forbid that I should do such a thing to my master, the Lord's anointed, or lift my hand against him; for he is the anointed of the Lord. With these words David rebuked his men and did not allow them to attack Saul. And Saul left the cave and went on his way." 1 Samuel 24:2-7

God had a plan for David's life but it wasn't God's timing yet for that plan to be put into place. What protection God provided though!!! Can you imagine running for your life and hiding out in a cave so deep that someone sitting alone on a rock at the front of the cave couldn't even hear you and your men?? Trust Him to work the same way in your life and the life of your prodigal. Let's read on and see how God actually used this cave encounter to David's advantage.

"Then David went out of the cave and called out to Saul, "My lord the king!" When Saul looked behind him, David bowed down and prostrated himself with his face to the ground. 'This day you have seen with your own eyes how the LORD delivered you into my hands in the cave. Some urged me to kill you, but I spared you; I said, 'I will not lay my hand on my lord, because he is the LORD's anointed.'

"(David speaking:) "See, my father, look at this piece of your robe in my hand! I cut off the corner of your robe and did not kill you. Now understand and recognize that I am not guilty of wrongdoing or rebellion. I have not wronged you, but you are hunting me down to take my life...When David finished saying this, Saul asked, 'Is this your voice David, my son?' And he wept aloud. 'You are more righteous than I,' he said. 'You have treated me well but I have treated you badly. You have just now told me of the good you did to me; the Lord delivered me into your hands and you did not kill me....May the Lord reward you well for the way you treated me today." 1 Samuel 24:8-11, 16-19. Then the chase was over.

God not only protected David but he allowed David to gain respect from his pursuer because of his actions. Expect the same. Protection and an awakening. Don't forget...God is still in the miracle working business. Praise him even before you know what is going on.

Several years ago a dear friend of mine was staying with us for a time of respite. One evening she had gone out to dinner with an 'old acquaintance'. We were expecting her back at our house by midnight or so. However, when I woke up at 1 AM, I realized she wasn't home yet. I tried calling her phone every hour and there was never any answer. I started praying through each hour as they ticked by with no word from her. All I knew to pray for was her safety and protection.

After about seven agonizing hours, we finally got word that she and her 'old friend' had been picked up by the local police for public intoxication and she was placed in a holding cell at the local jail to sober up. What incredible protection! She was actually alone in a jail cell during all those hours I was praying simply for protection. She couldn't have been safer--alone and surrounded by concrete. God was protecting her from others as well as from herself as she was in no condition to drive.

Praise Him in advance for protection!!

Prayer for the prodigal:
God almighty, You are El Roi, the God who sees. You know the best possible protection for (__). I praise You in advance for keeping a miraculous hedge of protection around (__). Also help (__) see You at work in their life as You place them in protection within their current situation.

Life verse:
"Haggai answered God by name, praying to the God who spoke to her, "You're the God who sees me!" Genesis 16:13

Personal Prayers and Thoughts:

Day 22
Praise for God's Plan

Meditation moment and prayer:
Father God, I thank you that your plans are bigger and more comprehensive than I can imagine. Thank you for not giving up on us when we fail to follow your plans consistently. Help me today to praise you for your patience as you work all your plans out for our lives. When we get busy wandering and worrying, please forgive us and bring us back to your plan for our lives.

**Do not forget this today:
God has a plan to use you and your prodigal.**

Often prodigals are just people who are running from God's calling and plan for their life. Jonah's story is a great example of someone running as far away from God's calling as possible. However God persistently continued to burden Jonah with this calling. "The word of the Lord came to Jonah…'Go to the great city of Ninevah and preach against it, because its wickedness has come up before me.' But Jonah ran away from the Lord and headed to Tarshish. He went down to Joppa where he found a ship headed to that port. After paying the fare, he went aboard and sailed to Tarshish to flee from the Lord.

"But the Lord hurled a powerful wind over the sea, causing a violent storm that threatened to break the ship apart. Fearing for their lives, the desperate sailors shouted to their gods for help and threw the cargo overboard to lighten the ship. But all this time Jonah was sound asleep down in the hold. So the captain went down after him. "How can you sleep at a time like this?" he shouted. "Get up and pray to your god! Maybe he will pay attention to us and spare our lives."...And since the storm was getting worse all the time, they asked him, "What should we do to you to stop this storm?" 'Throw me into the sea.' Jonah said, 'and it will become calm again. I know that this terrible storm is all my fault." Jonah 1:1-12

You know the drill. You feel a calling on your life in some way; perhaps it's just taking a meal to a sick family or reaching out to someone who needs a friend. But you just did not get it done...the busyness of life got in the way. Your own selfish ambitions take priority and all of a sudden you too are running from God.

God has a plan to use you and your prodigal but for whatever reason, you buy a ticket on the ship of selfishness and try to reach the coast of "I don't want to". However, it usually is a pretty miserable trip. Things begin to happen that make you uncomfortable and frustrated. Just like Jonah, you can even end up somewhere you least expect.

Like in Jonah's story, God is patiently waiting for you to come back to Him and fulfill His plan. When Jonah finally came to his senses and decided to follow God's will for his life (while he was in the belly of the whale which is a most unlikely place to find peace with God), amazing things happened. An entire city of 120,000 people repented of their sin and turned their eyes to God for forgiveness. Could God have used someone else to complete the task? Of course He could but He wanted to use Jonah to help him grow in his faith and knowledge of God. (Read Jonah 3:4-10.)

What grace!! What mercy!! God showed both Jonah and the people of Nineveh his incomprehensible mercy and deliverance. That is love.

Prayer for the prodigal:
Lord God creator of our lives, I praise you for having a purpose for (___)'s life. Once again thank you for knowing the beginning and the end of his/her story. I thank you in advance for all of these seemingly endless bad decisions and heartache knowing that You are at work in their life right now, even in the middle of this mess.

Even after years of exile and turmoil in our lives, you do promise in Jeremiah 29:11-14 that "I know the plans I have for you,' declares the Lord. 'Plans to prosper you and not to harm you, plans to give you a hope and a future." I am trusting in that today for (___) 's life.

Life verse:
"I know the plans I have for you,' declares the Lord. Plans to prosper you and not to harm you, plans to give you a hope and a future."
Jeremiah 29:11

Personal Prayers and Thoughts:

Day 23
Praying for People in Your Prodigal's Life Now

Meditation moment and prayer:
Lord I have at times been very critical of the relationships (__) keeps. Please give me a heart of compassion for those people who touch (__)'s life on a regular basis, i.e. their friends, co-workers, supervisors, and colleagues. I lift each of these people up to you today. Help me remember they are created by You and are somehow a part of the plan that You have for (__).

> **Remember this:**
> **God can use anything/anyone**
> **to draw us back to HIMSELF!**

When my daughter was about 15 years old, she was very interested in a boy from another town. I could tell however that this relationship was a little more one sided as they rarely saw each other in person and he was older than her. I prayed for wisdom in dealing with the situation as this guy was not someone I really approved of for her to be in a relationship with. Since this was all going on in the days before cell phones and computers, their only real consistent way of communicating was through letters and an occasional phone call. (Being a single mother at the time, I could control how much time she spent on the phone with him because long distance calls were very expensive for my budget.) I prayed for this boy's salvation and how I should approach the subject with my daughter.

One day my daughter asked me to mail a letter to him. So I took her letter to the mailbox. Then God gave me a brilliant idea. I had promised her I would put it in the mailbox but I didn't promise to leave it there. I knew that disrupting their communication would probably limit the growth of the relationship.

I don't know if my scheme worked, but God was faithful to answer my prayers as the two of them parted ways. God is concerned about our earthly relationships. They all can be used as part of His plan for each of our lives. So it's vital that you pray daily for the people who are touching your prodigal's life right now. Continue to pray for someone to come into their life and speak God's truth in love to them.

Prayer for the prodigal:
All-knowing God I lift those who are touching (___)'s life today. Help them be someone who has a deep-seated faith in You and can draw him/her closer to You in a non-threatening way. I lift up everyone, even though I really don't like most of them, that (___) comes in contact with over the next few days and weeks. May (___) see YOU and hear Your voice somehow through those people.

Life verse:
""But I say to you who hear, love your enemies, do good to those who hate you, bless those who curse you, pray for those who mistreat you."
Luke 6:27-28

Day 24
Praying for the Path

Meditation moment and prayer:
Lord, I can be so judgmental of people. Please forgive me for this and give me a heart of mercy and love even when someone is walking a path that I think is wrong. Give me Your eyes of love for my prodigal and all who they come in contact with.

**Never forget to:
Show mercy.
Be tender with sinners,
but not soft on sin.**

The tiny book of Jude near the end of the Bible is only 25 verses long. Jude was the brother of James and he wrote this book as an encouragement to believers.

The Message version of Jude 20-25 reads like this: "But you, dear friends, carefully build yourselves up in this most holy faith by praying in the Holy Spirit, staying right in the center of God's love, keeping your arms open and outstretched, ready for the mercy of our master, Jesus Christ. Go easy on those who hesitate in the faith. Go after those who take the wrong way. Be tender with sinners, but not soft on sin.... And now to Him who can carry you on your feet, standing tall in His bright presence, fresh and celebrating – to our one God, our only Savior, through Jesus Christ our master, be glory, majesty, strength, and rule before all time and now and to the end of all time."

This reminds me of how we treat a toddler: tenderly correcting them if they make a mistake, helping them get up when they fall down (which is often) and protecting them from the dangers of life. We treat them with typically more gentleness since they have such limited experiences. Jude is reminding us here to do the same with those who are struggling in their faith. Show mercy. Simply love them.

Verse 25 tells us: "Now to Him who is able to keep you from stumbling and to make you stand in the presence of His glory blameless and with great joy..." what a powerful prayer!! Use it today to lift your prodigal up before God that his/her path today or this week will be protected by the most High God and that He will keep him/her from stumbling.

Prayer for the prodigal:
Lord I know You are able to keep (___) from stumbling and You can draw him/her back to You. Help me to be tender with sinners while hating the sin. Help me and others around (___) show mercy and light the way to Your glorious presence.

I give You all the praise and glory because I know that You are able to keep (___) from stumbling and You can make them stand in Your presence blameless with great joy!! I am trusting You for this success!!

Life verse:
"Now to Him who is able to keep you from stumbling and to make you stand in the presence of His glory blameless and with great joy..." Jude 25

Day 25
Praying for Prodigal's Spiritual Sight

Meditation moment and prayer:
Lord sometimes my spiritual sight is so limited. Help me to remember that You are bigger than anything I can imagine or envision. I pray that I can see outside the little box I put You in so often. I also ask that You cause (___)'s spiritual eyes to be opened to see You in a new way.

**Consider this:
The Holy Spirit gives spiritual insight
in the most unexpected ways.**

Remember when it seemed like your mother had eyes in the back of her head? Just as you were getting ready to stick your hand in the cookie jar or pick up that interesting glass tea cup on the counter, your mother (who had been nowhere in sight two seconds before) would yell out, "Don't touch that!!!" Usually it would startle you so much that you immediately drew your hand back and looked around to see where that voice had come from. How did she know you were getting ready to do that? How could she see when she wasn't even in the room?

Honestly after being a Mom for more than 30 years, I can tell you it isn't that you have grown eyes in the back of your head literally. It is, however, that your perceptions and expectations change as you get to know your child intimately. As my daughter grew, I knew she never liked to stay in bed. So once we would put her down for sleep, I expected the pitter-patter of little feet coming from her room. Therefore, I knew (within about a 30 second variance) to say: "Get back in bed NOW," even though I wasn't anywhere near her room. I just knew her routines and preferences VERY WELL.

The same is true with our Heavenly Father. When we take time to get to know Him intimately, the eyes of our heart are opened to His wonders and preferences more clearly. When we take time to learn and stop expecting His reactions to be a certain way, the little box we often have placed Him in expands. At that point our faith grows also. We can begin to expect bigger things from Him and not be so surprised when He moves in new and mighty ways.

Prayer for the prodigal and life verse:
Lord, forgive me when My eyes are clouded by past hurts and grudges. Help me see (___) as You see him/her...as Your beloved child. I know You have a plan for their life and all of this hurt and heartache will someday be used for Your purpose and glory. Teach me to continue to expect great things. Use this time also to teach him/her in a new way. I pray the scripture prayer over (___) from Ephesians 1:16-19a "I have not stopped giving thanks for you (___), remembering you in my prayers. I keep asking that the God of our Lord Jesus Christ, the glorious Father, may give you the spirit of wisdom and revelation so that you (___) may know Him better. I pray that the eyes of your heart may be enlightened in order that you may know the hope to which he has called you, the riches of his glorious inheritance...and the incomparably great power toward us who believe..."
Ephesians 1:16-19a

Day 26
Praying for Prodigal's Physical Safety

Meditation moment and prayer:
Psalm 27:5 says "For in the day of trouble He will keep me safe in His dwelling: He will hide me in the shelter of the sacred tent and set me high upon a rock." My prayer today is for physical safety and protection for (___). Lord, most days I don't know where he/she is or what they are doing. But I know You promise never to leave us. So right now I ask for physical protection.

Remember this:
Do not let the 'what-ifs' haunt you!
God sees and protects!

Every day we are all traveling, driving, walking, etc to various places. We tend to think nothing is going to happen to cause us harm. Then...out of the blue, we get hit, fall or are in an accident in some way.

It happened to me recently. My husband, Jay and I were walking up a sidewalk. Nothing was happening out of the ordinary. Just walking. Somehow my foot slipped off the side of the sidewalk and the next thing I knew, I was falling. It was like slow motion to me. I felt my chin hit the concrete and then the glasses over my right eye. Next I felt the grass on my face and I was thinking to myself... "I'm falling...oh...gosh...I need to quit rolling down this hill." (There was a slight embankment there.) I did nothing wrong. I just stepped wrong. But I ended up with two broken bones in my left wrist and a broken bone in my left foot. The wrist required surgery and took several months to heal.

A few months later my nephew was visiting a friend's apartment. He stepped out on a fire escape which immediately collapsed. He ended up having severe brain injuries and will be changed for the rest of his life. He did nothing wrong to cause the accident. But he has to live with the consequences of the damage that was caused including now being blind in his right eye.

The 'What ifs' can haunt us. What if Jay & I had not gone for that walk? What if my nephew had just gone home for dinner that night instead of hanging out with friends? Once your loved one is grown or on their own, you cannot make sure they are always safe and out of harm's way. But we can pray for safety and protection. Remember God's ways are much higher and bigger than ours so He can protect and shelter. Be sure to praise Him for the protection He has provided so many times.

Prayer for the prodigal:
Lord God, you are El Roi, the God who sees. You see danger, our intentions, our steps and our path. Please go before, behind and surround (___) with your protection and watchful eye during the coming days. Through this protection please allow (___) to see Your hand working in their life in a real and confirming way. I give you praise now for all the safety and protection You constantly give us. Thank You for being El Roi, the God who sees and the God who protects. As King David proclaims in Ps 139:3 "You (Lord) see me when I travel and when I rest at home. You know everything I do." Thank you God for seeing and protecting.

Life verse:
"You (Lord) see me when I travel and when I rest at home. You know everything I do." Psalm 139:3

Personal Prayers and Thoughts:

Day 27
Praying for Prodigal's Emotions

Meditation moment and prayer:
Psalm 139:2 reminds me that You Lord are concerned with our emotions. "You know when I sit and when I rise; You perceive my thoughts from afar." Jesus even showed emotion. Lord I ask as I work through today, You would help me keep my emotions in check and aligned with Your will. Sometimes I get so hurt and angry with things (___) does or says that I just don't keep my cool.

> **Focus on this fact:**
> **God KNOWS us.**
> **He created all of us so He knows both**
> **you and your prodigal intimately.**

Recently, while being on active duty with the US Navy, my son was deployed several times off the coast of Somalia. Their ship would be gone for 6-9 months at a time. Communication during those deployments was very limited. They were often deployed during all the major "family" holidays, i.e. Thanksgiving and Christmas.

The first Christmas my son was deployed, I was very worried about his emotional state being so far away from home for that holiday. I had sent him and his shipmates multiple packages of holiday goodies several weeks before the holidays. But those packages got held up on a dock in Bahrain for several months, so the goodies I sent didn't make it to him in time to be enjoyed over Christmas.

As the holiday approached, I began sincerely praying for my son and the emotions of him and his shipmates. "Lord," I asked, "please make it possible for all of them to have a 'nice' Christmas, even without all the gifts that were in route." I prayed and prayed my son wouldn't get too homesick or upset with the current situation.

Later, my son told me that one of his shipmates had received some Christmas goodies on time. This shipmate had actually shared some very simple gifts for all of them to 'open' that Christmas Day. My son said those little trinkets that his friend shared allowed them all to celebrate together out in the middle of the ocean. This lifted their spirits during a tough time to be away from family. God heard my prayer and touched his emotions in just the way he needed that day. (For that I am eternally grateful).

He KNOWS us. God created all of us so He knows both you and your prodigal intimately. He gave us emotions for a reason. He can fully meet the emotional needs of our day to day lives if we trust Him for that.

Prayer for the prodigal:
Father God, reach down in Your loving wisdom and meet the emotional needs of (___) today. Show Yourself strong to them through whatever emotional distress they are dealing with now. Draw their heart back to You through this distress. Thank You that (___) is fearfully and wonderfully made.

Life verse:
"You (God) saw me before I was born and scheduled each day of my life before I began to breathe. Every day was recorded in your book!"
Psalm 139:16

Personal Prayers and Thoughts:

Day 28
Shine with Persistent Unconditional Love

Meditation moment and prayer:
Father God as Paul taught us in Romans 15:1-6, help me be more thoughtful in bearing with the shortcomings of (___) who is weaker in their faith than I am. Please give me a spirit of unity so that with one heart and one mouth I will bring glory to you, God and Father of our Lord Jesus Christ.

Remember this today:
Accept one another just as Christ accepted you.

As my children were growing up, they would often vent and express their frustrations at me. When they would get frustrated with things at school or work, I was the one they would call and complain to or get mad at. A friend would often question why I let them get so upset whenever we talked. I explained to him that the reason that they were comfortable doing that (complaining to me or getting angry with me over something that really had nothing to do with me) was because they knew I would always love them unconditionally...no matter what. I was persistent in my love for them. It was not conditional on their being nice to me all the time. I gave them a 'safe harbor' to vent and complain with my persistent love.

The same applies to our Heavenly Father. He wants us to come with our requests, our joys and our frustrations. We have to be comfortable enough with Him to know that He's going to love us unconditionally always no matter what our attitude.

Persistent love does not mean that we like everything people do. It does not mean that we become their doormat to wipe their dirty emotional shoes on constantly. It does mean that they can always trust us as parents or friends to be there in the good times and the bad. We are not fickle or whimsical in our love for them. We still expect respect and the best out of them. But having persistent, unconditional love means putting up with all of it so that they know, for sure, they always have a place of refuge to come back to. This is just like a light which shines no matter what the weather's doing. When it's beautiful and 75° out or when the hurricane winds are whirling and rain is coming down in torrents or the snow is piling up, the light continues to shine. That is unconditional, persistent love.

Paul puts it like this in Romans 15:1-7 "We who are strong ought to bear with the failings of the weak and not to please ourselves. Each of us should please his neighbor for his good, to build him up. For even Christ did not please himself but, as it is written: 'The insults of those who insult you have fallen on me.' For everything that was written in the past, was written to teach us, so that through endurance and the encouragement of the Scriptures we might have hope. May the God who gives endurance and encouragement give you a spirit of unity among yourselves as you follow Christ Jesus, so that with one heart and mouth you may glorify the God and Father of our Lord Jesus Christ. Accept one another, then, just as Christ accepted you, in order to bring praise to God."

Prayer for the prodigal:
Lord, forgive my unwillingness to accept (___) as he/she is. Help me retrain my focus to be more hopeful and accepting of (___) right where they are today rather than where I think they "should" be. Continue to grow me in Your hope for their life.

Life verse:
"May the God who gives endurance and encouragement give you a spirit of unity among yourselves as you follow Christ Jesus, so that with one heart and mouth you may glorify the God and Father of our Lord Jesus Christ. Accept one another, then, just as Christ accepted you, in order to bring praise to God." Romans 15:5-7

Personal Prayers and Thoughts:

Day 29
Be Attentive...Pray Without Ceasing

Meditation moment and prayer:
"O Lord, God of heaven, the great and awesome God, who keeps His covenant of love with those who love Him and obey His commands, let Your ear be attentive and Your eyes open to hear the prayer Your servant is praying before you day and night for (___). I confess the sins we, including myself in my father's house, have committed against You. We have acted very wickedly toward You. We have not obeyed the commands, decrees and laws You gave Your servant Moses. O Lord, let Your ear be attentive to the prayer of this Your servant and to the prayer of Your servants who delight in revering Your name. Give Your servant success today by granting him favor..." Nehemiah 1:5-7, 11

**Make this your focus today:
Prayer is simply talking with and
listening to God in a personal way.**

The story of Nehemiah in chapter 1 shows us how someone is willing to repent of sin for other people because of his love for those people. Nehemiah had found that the temple in Jerusalem had been destroyed and he was praying for an opportunity to rebuild it. In verses 2-5 he pleads for forgiveness on behalf of himself and his family and all of Israel because they had fallen away from the Lord. That is powerful ceaseless prayer!!!

What is prayer? Is it a requirement to be praying with your head bowed, eyes closed, in the church or in a closet? Prayer is simply communicating with our

Heavenly Father. Talking to him. Listening to him. Being in communication no matter what your stance or posture. God is all-knowing, all-seeing, and omnipotent. Therefore he doesn't require us to be in a certain dress, posture, or place. What He requires is that our attitude be humble before Him.

Are you willing to humble yourself before God on someone else's behalf as Nehemiah did?? That is power-filled praying. Search your heart today and ask God to show you how to better communicate with both Him and your prodigal.

Prayer for the prodigal and life verse:
Lord again I pray…"O Lord, God of heaven, the great and awesome God, who keeps his covenant of love with those who love him and obey his commands, let your ear be attentive and your eyes open to hear the prayer your servant is praying before you day and night for (___). I confess the sins we, including myself in my father's house, have committed against you. We have acted very wickedly toward you. We have not obeyed the commands, decrees and laws you gave your servant Moses. O Lord, let your ear be attentive to the prayer of this your servant and to the prayer of your servants who delight in revering your name. Give your servant success today by granting him favor…" Nehemiah 1:5-7, 11

Day 30
Seeing Light Gives Hope

Meditation moment and prayer:
Lord Jesus, I want to be someone who brings hope to the hopeless because I know how much anguish comes without it. There have been times when (___)'s situation seemed desperate. You have called us to an expectation in You that supersedes all the trials that life can throw at us. Help me to focus on that as it only comes from You.

> **Think on this:**
>   Hope is:
> **H-H**aving
> **O-O**utstanding
> **P-P**lans for
> **E-E**ternity

When my father was in his early 70's, he had a tragic accident. He fell at a doctor's office and broke his neck. He spent 13 days in the hospital paralyzed from the armpits down before God called him home to heaven. While those days were so incredibly hard for my dad, mother, sisters and I to endure, we had an amazing comfort which came from knowing without a doubt that my Dad had **H-O-P-E**.

He had the reassurance of the salvation that only comes from knowing Jesus personally. He had the faith that this earth and our earthly body is not our true home. Once we leave this physical realm of life and our body is no longer alive, we will have an eternal home in Heaven with God, our Heavenly Father and our Lord, Jesus Christ. Through this, we all could endure those dark days of sadness without despair.

As we were there in the intensive care unit with Dad, I noticed, through hearing the cries of others in the unit, that so many had a sense of true desperation. They are convinced that this life is all there is. Those in this situation were mourning in a completely different way...they were overcome with anguish. I could hear it in their cries and sense it in their grieving. How sad it is to have NO hope.

As a light shining in the darkness can give excitement and confidence to someone who has lost their way, so we can share this opportunity for optimism with a lost and desperate world.

Ephesians 3:17-19 is a powerful scripture prayer that the apostle Paul gave us regarding hope. "I keep asking that the God of our Lord Jesus Christ, the Glorious Father, may give you the Spirit of wisdom and revelation, so that you may know Him better. I pray also that the eyes of your heart may be enlightened in order that you may know the HOPE to which He has called you, the riches of His glorious inheritance in the saints, and His incomparably great power toward us who believe."

Say it as a prayer over and over inserting your own name and the name of your prodigal into the scripture. This is a tremendous prayer of power when you aren't sure how to pray.

Prayer for the prodigal and life verse:
I keep asking that You, God of our Lord Jesus Christ, the Glorious Father, may give (___) the Spirit of wisdom and revelation, so that they may know You better. I pray also that the eyes of (___)'s heart may be enlightened in order that they may know the HOPE to which You have called us, the riches of Your glorious inheritance in the Saints, and Your incomparably great power toward us who believe."
Ephesians 3:17-19

Personal Prayers and Thoughts:

Day 31
Sharper Than a Two-Edged Sword

Meditation moment and prayer:
Lord God please help me guard my words when I communicate with (___). Show me ways to let my light for You glow around all the conversations we have. Teach me scripture that will build up and reinforce the work You are doing in both of our lives. Help me remember this scripture as I work on communicating in a loving and merciful way. Sometimes it is so hard to love (___) and their friends through all the hurt and disappointment. But I'm trusting You are growing me into Your likeness through all of this as well.

Remember this:
God's word is living and active,
sharper than a two edged sword.

Hebrews 4:12 tells us that God's word is sharper than a two edged sword. We really don't use swords in our culture so this concept of a two edged sword may be foreign to us. I'm sure you have heard about or seen an original push lawn mower...the kind with no motor. You would push it around the yard with it's steel blades spinning as fast as you could push. However, the blades were only sharp on one side. You couldn't go backwards with that old mower because the blades were not sharp on the back side. Once motorized mowers were invented, they discovered that if both sides of the blades were sharp, grass cutting became much easier and more efficient (especially since we didn't have to push quite so hard!)

When using God's Word in conversation with others we must be very careful to not beat people 'over the head' with scripture as a way to condemn them. Remember a light is never judgmental. It just shines. Period. Over the past few weeks we have incorporated specific scripture prayers into your everyday meditation time and prayers

Scripture prayers are also very beneficial when we just don't know what or how to pray anymore. Since God deemed these scripture prayers worthy enough to be included in His Holy Word for our use, we should be compelled to read them, memorize them, and use them to call upon His name. In Psalm 119:11 the psalmist writes "I have hidden your word in my heart that I might not sin against You."

Here are some powerful scripture prayers for you to use (which can be found typed out in Appendix A):
- Ephesians 1:15-19
- Ephesians 3:14-21
- Philippians 1:9-11
- Colossians 1:9b-12
- Colossians 2:2-3
- 2 Thessalonians 1:11-12

I challenge you to personalize these as you memorize these scripture prayers. God's word is alive and moves hearts today if we are faithful to press into His presence with the Word He has given us.

Prayer for your prodigal:
Lord as I lean more and more into Your Word to find scripture prayers, please use them to bring glory to Yourself in both my life and the life of (___). Help me use scripture as a way of encouragement and wisdom. Also as You bring someone else into their life that loves You, please use Your words in their relationship as well. I know You are able to have all of our words coordinate in a perfect orchestration. I am trusting You for that.

Life verse:
"If any of you lacks wisdom, he should ask God, who gives generously to all without finding fault, and it will be given to him. But when he asks, he must believe and not doubt, because he who doubts is like a wave of the sea, blown and tossed by the wind." James 1:5-6

Personal Prayers and Thoughts:

Day 32
The Prodigal Revisited...the Outcome
The Light Shines On

Meditation moment and prayer:
Father God, I realize the story of the prodigal son is really about You and me. It shows how I have sinned against You always begging for things to go a certain way and 'wanting my inheritance now' without waiting on Your timing. You are the loving, ever vigilant Father watching and waiting for us to come back to You and repent. Thank You Father God for accepting me back with open arms. Help me to do the same with my prodigal. Teach me to be willing to eagerly await their return and celebrate it when it happens, just as the father did.

Let's revisit the prodigal son story and see how it ended. "Not long after that, the younger son got together all he had, set off for a distant country and there squandered his wealth in wild living. After he had spent everything, there was a severe famine in that whole country, and he began to be in need. So he went and hired himself out to a citizen of that country, who sent him to his fields to feed pigs. He longed to fill his stomach with the pods that the pigs were eating but no one gave him anything.
"When he came to his senses, he said, 'How many of my father's hired men have food to spare, and here I am starving to death! I will set out and go back to my father and say to him: Father, I have sinned against heaven and against you. I am no longer worthy to be called your son; make me like one of your hired men.' So he got up and went to his father.

"But while he was still a long way off, his father saw him and was filled with compassion for him; he ran to his son, threw his arms around him and kissed him.
"The son said to him, 'Father, I have sinned against heaven and against you. I am no longer worthy to be called your son.'
"But the father said to his servants, 'Quick! Bring the best robe and put it on him. Put a ring on his finger and sandals on his feet. Bring the fattened calf and kill it. Let's have a feast and celebrate. For this son of mine was dead and is alive again; he was lost and is found.' (Luke 15:13-24)

I think it is incredible how the father greeted the long lost son. He went running to him, kissed him and called for a huge celebration!!! What a response. Can you imagine being that excited especially after all the heartache the prodigal had put him through? Even the lost one was surprised. He was just going to ask to be hired as a servant but actually was given the royal treatment instead.

Will that be your response to your prodigal when they return? Will you be thrilled and shining your light brightly yet silently? Or will you be tempted to bring up the past and just be waiting for the next 'episode' to happen?

We can learn a lot from this father by examining what he did NOT do. He didn't shake his finger and say, "I told you this would happen." Or "I can't believe you are asking for something from me again...Look at the mess you have already made." He didn't stand on the front porch with his arms crossed and a condescending scowl on his face. In fact the father didn't even let the son get all the way up the drive!! He went running to meet him with open arms!!

**NEVER FORGET:
Your immediate reactions
to your prodigal are so critical.
You need to continue shining the light of Jesus
each time you encounter him/her.
Silently, continuously, enthusiastically
show them love.
The Heavenly Father does that for you...**

Prayer for a prodigal:
Lord, please strengthen me to be Your loving, silent, enthusiast light any time I am around (___). Help me remember the father's reactions and imitate them each time I have contact with (___). Thank You for loving each of us more than we deserve. Give me that compassion even through the heartache just as You have done for us. Thank you for the examples You have given. Help me to shine Your light in (___)'s darkness day by day.

Life verse:
"And this is my prayer: that your love may abound more and more in knowledge and depth of insight, so that you may be able to discern what is best and may be pure and blameless until the day of Christ, filled with the fruit of righteousness that comes through Jesus Christ – to the glory and praise of God." Philippians 1:9-11

Personal Prayers and Thoughts:

APPENDIX A

Scripture Prayer Section – these are samples of scripture prayers you can use for yourself and others when you just aren't sure what or how to pray.

Ephesians 1:15-19
"For this reason I too, having heard of the faith in the Lord Jesus which exists among you, and your love for all the saints, do not cease giving thanks for you, while making mention of you in my prayers; that the God of our Lord Jesus Christ, the Father of glory, may give to you a spirit of wisdom and of revelation in the knowledge of Him. I pray that the eyes of your heart may be enlightened, so that you may know what is the hope of His calling, what are the riches of the glory of His inheritance in the saints, and what is the surpassing greatness of His power toward us who believe."

Philippians 1:9-11
"And this I pray, that your love may abound still more and more in real knowledge and all discernment, so that you may approve the things that are excellent, in order to be sincere and blameless until the day of Christ; having been filled with the fruit of righteousness which comes through Jesus Christ, to the glory and praise of God.

Ephesians 3:14-21
"For this reason, I bow my knees before the Father, from whom every family in heaven and on earth derives its name, that He would grant you, according to the riches of His glory, to be strengthened with power through His Spirit in the inner man; so that Christ may dwell in your hearts through faith; and that you, being rooted and grounded in love, may be able to comprehend with all the saints what is the breadth and length and height and depth, and to know the love of Christ which surpasses knowledge, that you may be filled up to all the fullness of God. Now to Him who is able to do exceedingly abundantly beyond all that we ask or think, according to the power that works within us, to Him be the glory to all generations forever and ever. Amen."

Colossians 1:9b-12
"We have not ceased to pray for you and to ask that you may be filled with the knowledge of His will in all spiritual wisdom and understanding, so that you may walk in a manner worthy of the Lord, to please Him in all respects, bearing fruit in every good work and increasing in the knowledge of God; strengthened with all power, according to His glorious might, for the attaining of all steadfastness and patience; joyously giving thanks to the Father, who has qualified us to share in the inheritance of the saints in light."

Colossians 2:2-3
"I pray that their hearts may be encouraged, having been knit together in love, and attaining to all the wealth that comes from the full assurance of understanding, resulting in a true knowledge of God's mystery, that is, Christ Himself, in whom are hidden all the treasures of wisdom and knowledge."

2 Thessalonians 1:11-12
"To this end also we pray for you always that our God may count you worthy of your calling, and fulfill every desire for goodness and the work of faith with power; in order that the name of our Lord Jesus may be glorified in you, and you in Him, according to the grace of our God in the Lord Jesus Christ."

(These verses are from the New American Standard Translation Bible.)

Personal Prayers and Thoughts:

Personal Prayers and Thoughts:

www.ingramcontent.com/pod-product-compliance
Lightning Source LLC
Chambersburg PA
CBHW071705040426
42446CB00011B/1930